Wilma Rudolph

Run For Glory

Wilma Rudolph
Run For Glory

By LINDA JACOBS

EMC CORPORATION
ST. PAUL, MINNESOTA

Library of Congress Cataloging in Publication Data

Jacobs, Linda.
  Wilma Rudolph: run for glory

  (Her women who win 2)
  SUMMARY: A biography of the woman who overcame crip-
pling polio as a child to become the first woman to win
three gold medals in track in a single Olympics.
  1. Rudolph, Wilma, 1940-   — Juvenile literature.
2. Track-athletics for women — Juvenile literature.
[1. Rudolph, Wilma, 1940-   — 2. Track and field — Bio-
graphy] I. Title.
GV697.R8J32 796.4'2'0924 [B] [92] 74-31084
ISBN 0-88436-172-1
ISBN 0-88436-173-X pbk.

Published by EMC Corporation
180 East Sixth Street
St. Paul, Minnesota 55101
Printed in the United States of America
0 9 8 7 6 5 4 3 2 1

The huge crowd fell silent. All of Rome, Italy, seemed to hold its breath. Six teams waited to run for glory in the 1960 Olympics.

One girl stood out from the others. Wilma Rudolph had already won two gold medals. She had broken one world record and tied another. Now she would try for a third medal in the 400 meter relay. In moments, she might become the first American woman to win three gold medals in track in a single Olympics.

Could she do it? The crowd hoped so. They already loved this pretty black girl from Tennessee State University.

The starting runners lined up. Each gripped the baton that she hoped her team would carry to victory. "On your mark! Get set!" Crack! Runners shot from their blocks, as the starting gun sounded.

U.S. runner Martha Hudson led the field. She passed the baton to Barbara Jones. Barbara raced away and passed smoothly to Lucinda Williams. The U.S. team led! The crowd roared as Lucinda raced toward Wilma Rudolph. Wilma reached out for the baton.

One final winning stride, and Wilma lunged through the tape ahead of Jutta Heine to win the 400 meter relay for the U.S. women's team and a third first place Gold Medal for herself at the 1960 Olympics.

Lucinda let go too early! It nearly toppled to the ground. The crowd gasped and groaned, but Wilma didn't blink an eye. She stood still until she had the baton and then sped away. Jutta Heine of Germany raced ahead of her.

Wilma's heart pounded. Her breath came in great gasps. What an awful mistake! It could cost the race. Wilma kept so calm that reporters later called her "The Great Frozen Face." She didn't panic, she just turned on the speed. Her great strides gobbled ground until she pulled ahead of Jutta Heine and smashed through the tape.

Her perfect form and intense effort show as Wilma smashes through the tape to win the women's 200 meter for her second Gold Medal.

Wilma stood high and center at the awards ceremony after winning her first Gold Medal for the women's 100 meter dash in the 1960 Olympics. At left is Dorothy Hyman of Britain who came in second. At right is Giuseppina Leone of Italy who was third.

First place! Three gold medals for Wilma! Sixty thousand people went wild. Some of them yelled her Olympic nickname, "black gazelle." Others yelled her hometown nickname, "Skeeter." Still others yelled "Chattanooga Choo-Choo." Whatever they called her, they all cheered Wilma. They tossed autograph books, hats and programs onto the field.

Wilma ran down the sidelines to one special man — her coach, Edward Temple. "Thank you," she breathed, and cried happy tears.

That thank you wasn't just for Coach Temple. It was also for Wilma's family and her high school coach. It was

Waving the lucky straw hat she brought with her to the Olympics, Wilma smiles broadly with the other winners of the 200 meter dash. Jutta Heine (right) won the second place Silver Medal. Dorothy Hyman (left) won the third place Bronze Medal.

9

for a childhood friend named Bob Eldridge. Those people had helped, too. And they knew something that the cheering crowd didn't know. They knew that people had seen more than a great race. Sixty thousand onlookers had just seen a miracle!

Winning three gold medals was just icing on the cake for Wilma. She had already proved herself a champion, just by learning to walk.

Wilma was born on June 23, 1940, in Clarksville, Tennessee. Her family was poor. There were sixteen children already, Wilma was the seventeenth. Later, two more children were born.

Wilma weighed only four and a half pounds. She was sickly right from the start. When she had scarlet fever and pneumonia, her whole family thought she would die. But they held on and hoped. Tiny Wilma struggled through, but she was so weak that she had to stay in bed most of the time.

Then, when Wilma was four, came the worst thing of all. Polio! It left her with one leg crippled. The doctors said she would never walk.

Wilma's parents, Blanche and Eddie, couldn't believe that. They weren't the kind to give up because somebody said it couldn't be done. After all, people said a family couldn't raise all those children on the salary of a store clerk and a maid, but the Rudolphs were doing it.

11

Wilma was bending over in a position runners often use to relax their leg muscles, when a photographer took this shot of her long and lovely legs — legs thought hopelessly crippled by polio sixteen years before.

Blanche Rudolph decided to do the impossible for Wilma, too. She wrapped little Wilma in a blanket and took her 45 miles by bus to the Meharry Medical College in Nashville.

The doctors ran tests. They poked and prodded and shook their heads. Years of daily massage might save the leg, they said. They couldn't be sure.

A "might" was good enough for Mrs. Rudolph if that was all she could get. But there was a problem — she couldn't travel 90 miles round trip every day. She had other children, and she had to work.

"Teach me how to do it," she said. So the doctors taught her. And they worked out a plan. Mrs. Rudolph would massage Wilma's leg at home, and once every week, she would take Wilma to the clinic for special heat and water treatments.

Mrs. Rudolph went home and started the plan. She went to work and came home to fix dinner for her big family. Then she massaged Wilma's leg until bedtime. A year went by. The doctors tested Wilma again. There was only a tiny improvement.

"Maybe it just won't work," they said. But it had to work, Mrs. Rudolph told them. After all, there had been *some* improvement — that meant there could be more. They would have to try harder. That night, Mrs. Rudolph started teaching three older children how to

massage Wilma's leg. Everybody pitched in — they worked in four shifts.

It seemed like most of the time Wilma had someone fussing over her leg. Sometimes she got tired of it and cried. Sometimes she didn't believe that it would help at all. But she wasn't sad very often — mostly, she kept up her courage.

In "Olympic Village", a group of shops set up specially for the Olympic games, Wilma visited the shoe store for track shoes, and made friends with the Italian cooks in the cafeteria.

Those were glorious, unforgettable days for Wilma in Rome, 1960. Reporters from all over the world wanted to record her story.

She would lie in bed or sit in her favorite chair, and watch the other children play. Wilma couldn't run with them, but she could laugh and talk with them. From her chair, she shared everything that happened in the Rudolph household.

By the time she was six, she was taking a more active part in things. The treatments were working — Wilma could almost walk! She'd hop around the house, and often she'd fall, but Wilma only laughed and got back up.

She kept trying and she kept getting better. When she was eight the clinic doctors gave her a leg brace. Wilma practiced walking with it — she worked hard and did well. Soon the doctors gave her a special high-topped shoe. Wilma still limped, but she could get around well enough to go to school.

She could also get around well enough to play basketball. Her brother, Westley, mounted a peach basket on a pole so he and the other Rudolph boys could play basketball. But Wilma had other ideas. She shocked Westley and the rest of the family when she started to play — dribbling and shooting and running the best she could. The boys couldn't play without her — Wilma was always there, ready to go. She was so ready that she would play alone after the boys got tired.

One day, Mrs. Rudolph came home from work and looked out in the back yard where Wilma was shooting baskets. But something was unusual. The special shoe was gone — Wilma was playing barefoot! Wilma Rudolph never again wore her special shoe. She could walk like anyone else.

Wilma ran and played and loved every minute of it. She loved people, too, and they loved her. Wilma had

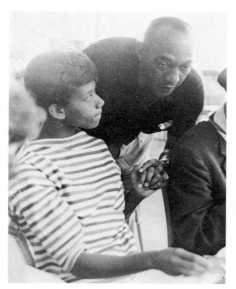

At Olympic Village Wilma met another great American Olympic runner from the past — Jesse Owens.

lots of friends in school — one of those friends was Bob Eldridge. He liked Wilma because she played and ran as good as the boys, and the two of them played basketball together all through elementary school.

When Wilma and Bob went to high school, both of them kept on playing basketball. Bob made the boys' varsity; Wilma made the girls' team. Coach Clinton Gray was glad to have her. He loved to watch her play, dashing and darting around the court.

Once, as he was standing close to the sidelines, Wilma charged over the court dribbling the ball as fast as she could. She didn't watch where she was going, and smashed into Coach Gray, toppling in a heap at his feet.

17

"You're just a skeeter," he said, as he laughed and helped her up. Wilma looked at him, wondering what he meant. The coach laughed again. She buzzed all over the place, he told Wilma, just like a mosquito.

"I'll call you Skeeter," he said. The nickname stuck. Soon, everybody in school called Wilma "Skeeter." They used the name with affection. Everyone was proud of Wilma. By the time she was fifteen, she was an all-state basketball player. She had set a Burt High School record by scoring 803 points in 25 games.

And, though she didn't know it, she had been noticed by an important man. Ed Temple, the track coach at Tennessee State, saw Wilma playing basketball. But he hardly noticed all the baskets she made. Instead, he watched the way she moved.

"She could be a runner," he told Coach Gray, and Coach Gray agreed. When Coach Temple left that evening, he had convinced Coach Gray to start a girls' track team at Burt High School.

Wilma was one of the team's first members. In practice, Coach Gray timed her running. He could hardly believe his stopwatch. Indeed, Wilma Rudolph could be a runner — a great one. Coach Gray saw it and Wilma proved it later. She went to a state high school meet, where she ran in the 50, 75, and 100 yard dashes. She walked away with first prize in all three.

19

Wilma was on her way. She worked hard at running, and kept winning meets. She also kept up with other things — she made a B+ average in school.

Her family said that school and even running weren't really Wilma's favorite activities. What she really liked to do was sleep. Wilma could even sleep right before a big meet.

She slept so much that her family teased her and said she was lazy. She overslept almost every morning, until she had to scurry to school so she wouldn't be late for practice. But oversleeping didn't hurt Wilma's running. She was winning so much that she surprised everyone — everyone but Coach Ed Temple of Tennessee State, who wasn't surprised at all. He had expected great things from Wilma, and he had plans for her.

Those plans centered around the "Tigerbelles" — the women's track team. Coach Temple had spent many hours building the team. He kept the women practicing all through the school year, and he went with them to meets. In the summers, he tried out promising high school girls. Those who made the team earned scholarships to college.

He invited Wilma to try out in the summer after her junior year. Wilma was so excited she could hardly breathe. The whole Rudolph family was excited. A college scholarship! If Wilma made the Tigerbelles, she would get more than a chance to run. She would get an education that her family couldn't possibly afford.

"If running can get you a scholarship, don't ever give up," Wilma's mother said. Wilma nodded. She remembered the long years as a cripple. Her family hadn't given up then, and she hadn't given up. She wasn't about to start now.

Wilma went to the Tennessee State campus with high hopes. She dreamed of being a runner on the famous Tigerbelles. She dreamed of studying to become a teacher.

On the first day of tryouts, those dreams got ragged around the edges. Coach Temple lined up Wilma and nine other girls. He gave them their first orders — jog five miles through rough farmland. The girls all tried. Wilma fell several times. But she got up and tried again. She made it back to the finish line with the others.

The next day, Wilma had to get up at five o'clock. She staggered out to the track, still sleepy. Five A.M. is awfully early for a girl who liked her sleep almost as much as she liked running.

To make things worse, Wilma had to run against one of the top Tigerbelles. She lined up with the others. The gun cracked, and Wilma shot away, but the other girl ran better. She passed Wilma so fast that she seemed to be only a blur. Wilma finished over five yards behind.

Wilma went off by herself and cried. Why had she bothered to come? She was sure she had lost her chance at the team and the scholarship. But all the tears and the doubts didn't make her quit. She went back the next day and tried again. And she lost again.

Wilma had become so famous that she was even invited to the White House to meet President Kennedy. Her mother, Mrs. Blanche Rudolph, is seated on the right.

Wilma could see herself going home in disgrace. She thought of her family, of Coach Gray and Bob Eldridge. They all believed in her. They would all be so disappointed. For the first time, the girl who had conquered polio felt like a failure.

But Coach Temple didn't think she was a failure. He hadn't expected a high school girl to be as good as his crack Tigerbelles. He was looking for promising talent, not polished performance. He had seen that talent earlier in Wilma, and he still saw it. He also saw Wilma's determination — how she kept going even when she was hurt and discouraged. She could be a winner.

24

As a member of the Tigerbelles, Ed Temple's famous track team from Tennessee State, Wilma won awards in track meets all over the country.

Wilma couldn't believe it when she got her scholarship. She was going to be a Tigerbelle! She hadn't failed after all. Of course, Wilma was happy. When she went home to Clarksville, she celebrated with her family. But something still bothered her. Beneath her victory smiles, Wilma worried. True, she had gotten her scholarship, and she wasn't about to turn it down. But she still wondered if she could ever be as good as the experienced Tigerbelles.

"Quit wondering," her mother said. "Work!" Wilma did — she worked so hard that she qualified for the 1956 Olympics during her senior year in high school.

Wilma went to Melbourne, Australia, where she ran in the 400 meter relay team and brought home a bronze medal. With just over a year of training, Wilma had helped her team win third place.

All the Rudolphs celebrated. Bob Eldridge made sure that everyone in Clarksville knew of Wilma's win, he broadcast the news all over town. But even though Wilma was a heroine to her family and friends, she wasn't to herself. She still had to prove herself on the Tigerbelles at Tennessee State. Until she did that, she wouldn't be happy, she wouldn't feel like a champion.

The work was just beginning. Wilma graduated from high school in June. She walked proudly beside Bob Eldridge — grinning at him and feeling strange in her cap with its floppy tassel. Her high school years were over. Now she'd start a grown-up life away from home.

Wilma graduated from Tennessee State in May, 1963. Odd as it seems, it is somehow fitting that Wilma should be holding an armful of track shoes with her diploma. It was track that won her a college scholarship — and world fame.

Wilma was glad that Bob Eldridge would be a familiar part of that life. He was going to Tennessee State, too. He would play basketball on the varsity team. Everybody at Burt High School had great hopes for Bob and for Wilma, and those hopes were not in vain. Bob made All-American in basketball.

Wilma ran for glory. She practiced hard every day. She even ran when she wanted to sleep. Coach Temple pushed her hard, and Wilma always gave him the performance he wanted. She quickly became one of his four top runners. He was so proud of her that he used her as an example for his new runners. But one thing bothered him.

He knew that Wilma had the spirit of a champion and she had the talent. After constant coaching, she had the technique. She should be the fastest runner on the Tigerbelles.

But she wasn't. The three other top Tigerbelles always beat her. Coach Temple couldn't understand it. Neither could Wilma.

Sometimes she thought she just wasn't as good a runner as everyone thought. Maybe she really was only fourth best — maybe that's all she could be.

Wilma kept trying and wondering and coming in fourth. Then, one chilly fall day, she got a sore throat. She gargled and forgot about it, but it kept getting worse. When Wilma got a fever, Coach Temple took her to a doctor. The doctor only looked at Wilma for a few minutes, but he knew what was wrong — her tonsils would have to come out. They had been draining her strength for years.

Wilma had the operation, and recovered quickly. When she started to run again, nobody could beat her.

Other awards came quickly to Wilma after her fantastic Olympic achievement. She was awarded this 1961 Sullivan Award as the outstanding amateur athlete in America — only the third woman in 31 years to receive the coveted prize given each year by the Amateur Athletic Union.

In 1959, Wilma started her record-smashing route at the Rome Olympics. She won one meet after another and qualified easily for the 1960 Olympics.

Her three gold medals set the whole world cheering. Wilma was a heroine to everybody. More important, she was a heroine to herself. She had done what she set out to do. Her high-school doubts were gone.

There was a rush to honor Wilma. Her hometown of Clarksville held a parade for her. She won the James E. Sullivan Memorial Trophy. Only two women had won it before her. They were swimmers. Wilma was the first woman runner to win this trophy honoring her outstanding sportsmanship.

Wilma loved the honors. She loved standing at the top of the sports world. But she knew that all the fame had changed her life. She was still the same in many ways. She loved her family and hometown friends. She kept up with her studies. She still liked sleeping almost as much as running.

But she was only twenty years old and she had already gone to the top of the sports world. She had done the running. She had won the glory. Now what? Where could she go from the top?

Another girl might have gone into a slump. She might have decided that she'd done all there was to do. No new challenges lay ahead.

Wilma was too wise to do that. Life was just beginning for her. She kept busy, running in other meets, planning her career in teaching. Soon she graduated from Tennessee State.

And she got married. Lots of boys had liked Wilma, but she hadn't had time to date many of them. There was only one boy she always had time to see — Bob Eldridge.

Wilma married him after they graduated from Tennessee State. They planned an active future together — Bob went to work as an engineer, and Wilma taught junior high school. Soon they started a family, and Wilma found a quieter glory in her work, her husband, and her children.

With Bob, Wilma went back to the Olympics to Munich, Germany, in 1972, this time as a television commentator, reporting on the same races she won in 1960.

Today Wilma and Bob live in Chicago with their children. Above, starting at the left, are Yolanda, Djuana, Wilma, Xurry, and Robert, Jr. (known as Dude). Yolanda is a track star in her own right, and, coached by her mother, she might someday go to the Olympics too.

Today, Wilma Rudolph Eldridge has four children, Yolanda, Djuana, Robert, and Xurry. She tries to give them the same kind of love that she knew as a child. She tries to show her pride when they do well and understand when they make mistakes.

She is proud enough to want them to do their best. She is wise enough not to flaunt her own accomplishments. During her running days Wilma won over two hundred trophies and medals, but she doesn't display them in her home. She thinks that would be

Wilma shares a quiet, sleepy moment with Xurry.

Bob asked Wilma to bring out some of her trophies for the photographer. Wilma doesn't like to display them in their home. In fact, she has given many of them away.

unfair to her children. They have their own lives to live, and they shouldn't have to do it in the shadow of a famous mother.

Wilma's wisdom makes her a good mother to her own children. It also makes her good at working with other children. When she taught junior high for eight years, she talked to her students — she took an interest in them. She tried to help.

Wilma is no longer a classroom teacher. But she is still trying to help children. She is Assistant Director of the Youth Foundation in Chicago, where she coaches the foundation's women's track team. As a coach, she tries to be like Ed Temple. She cares about her girls, and about the sport of track. Wilma wants to turn her girls into the best possible runners. She wants them to work, to win, and most of all, to run for glory.

For many years Wilma was a teacher in junior high school. Today, she still works with children — this time as Assistant Director of the Youth Foundation in Chicago.

Now Wilma takes as much pleasure giving trophies as she once did winning them. Here, she and Mayor Richard Daley of Chicago present an award to the winner of the 10,000 meter walk.

She knows they can't win all the time. Every girl can't be a champion. But she also knows that every girl can do her best, and Wilma won't let them settle for less than that. She knows she'd be cheating them if she did.

She knows because she remembers all the people who insisted on her best, who wouldn't let her settle for

37

less. Her mother wouldn't let her settle for less than walking normally. In high school, Coach Gray wouldn't let her stop until she played All-State basketball. In college, Coach Temple wouldn't let her be less than the Tigerbelles' top runner. Wilma wouldn't let herself settle for less than three gold medals in a single Olympics.

Giving her best every time put Wilma Rudolph on top of the sports world when she was twenty. It gave her new worlds to conquer when the medals were only a memory.

Now giving her best keeps Wilma active with a career and a family. It also keeps her interested in the wider sports world. Wilma hosted T.V. specials on Olympic athletes. She speaks before large groups. She went back to the Olympics to Munich, Germany, where she helped with T.V. coverage of the Olympics in 1972. She saw other young girls running the same events that she ran in 1960.

March 14, 1974, was to be a very important date in Wilma's life. It was the day she was inducted into the new Black Athletes Hall of Fame. She is one of only three women included. It was one of the proudest, happiest days in her life. She doesn't miss the old, run-for-glory days. She is busy, and happy with her life. Of course, things have changed. She is a coach instead of a runner. She is a grown woman instead of a young girl.

Yet in one way, things are much the same. She still loves her sleep and she still doesn't have enough time for it. She is a career woman, a coach, a speaker, a television personality, a wife, and a mother.

Wilma Rudolph is no longer a high school girl crashing into her coach. She is no longer an Olympic athlete. But she's still busy doing her best. She's still a skeeter.

Wilma (left) hosted her own Olympic Special on TV. Her guests are Wyomia Tyus, Ollie Matson and Donna DeVerona.

PHOTO CREDITS

Giuliano Bevilacqua: 12, 14, 15, 17, 34

Black Star (Scheler): 21

NCT (Ron Nielsen): Cover, 9 (bottom), 32, 35, 36, 37, (Roland M. Charles) 39

United Press International Photos: 8 (bottom), 9 (right), 10, 23, 25, 28, 31

Wide World Photos: 6, 8, (left), 18, 26

Black Widow
Spiders

ABDO
Publishing Company
A Buddy Book
by
Julie Murray

Published by Buddy Books, an imprint of ABDO Publishing Company, 4940 Viking Drive, Suite 622, Edina, Minnesota 55435. Copyright © 2002 by Abdo Consulting Group, Inc. International copyrights reserved in all countries. No part of this book may be reproduced in any form without written permission from the publisher.

Printed in the United States.

Edited by: Christy DeVillier
Contributing Editors: Matt Ray, Michael P. Goecke
Graphic Design: Maria Hosley
Image Research: Deborah Coldiron
Cover Photograph: Ronald Billings (www.forestryimages.org)
Interior Photographs: Ronald Billings, Michael A Kelly (www.wildlifenature.com), Mark Kostich (www.kostich.com)

Library of Congress Cataloging-in-Publication Data

Murray, Julie, 1969-
  Black widow spiders/Julie Murray.
     p. cm. — (Animal kingdom)
  Summary: Briefly describes the physical characteristics, behavior and habitat of the poisonous black widow spider.
  ISBN 1-57765-728-4
     1. Black widow spider—Juvenile literature. [1. Black widow spider. 2. Spiders.] I. Title. II. Animal kingdom (Edina, Minn.)

QL458.42.T54 M85 2002
595.4'4—dc21

2001046454

Contents

Arachnids

Spiders have been around about 400 million years. There are more than 35,000 kinds of spiders. Some people think that spiders are insects. They are wrong. Spiders are arachnids. Arachnids are small animals with eight legs and two body parts.

Spiders are arachnids.

"Black widow" is a common name for some kinds of widow spiders. Widow spiders are cobweb weavers. Cobweb weavers build a tangled cobweb from their silk. The black widow's silk is strong. It is stronger than most other arachnid's silk.

Amazing Strength of Spider Silk

A pencil-thick thread of spider silk can stop a Boeing 747 jet flying at full speed.

Polynesian fishermen used spider silk as fishing line.

Some tribes in New Guinea used spider webs as rain hats.

In 1709, a Frenchman, Bon de Saint-Hilaire, made socks and gloves from spider silk.

The Poisonous Female

Maybe you have heard that the black widow spider is poisonous. This is true for the female. The female black widow has venom. Venom is poison. The female kills prey with this venom. She also uses her venom when she is in danger. A black widow's venom can hurt people, too.

Male

Female

Male black widow spiders are not
poisonous like the females.

Size And Color

   The female black widow is the largest of the cobweb weavers. With her legs spread, she can be over one inch (two cm) long. This arachnid is shiny black. There is a bright red hourglass mark on her abdomen. An hourglass looks like this: ⧖

   The male black widow is smaller. It is mostly brown. He has white and reddish marks on his sides.

Body Parts

Like all arachnids, black widows have two main body parts. The front part is the cephalothorax (sef-uh-luh-thor-acks). The cephalothorax houses the brain, eyes, mouth, and stomach. The black widow's back part is the abdomen. The heart and lungs are inside the abdomen. Spinnerets are on the tip of the abdomen. Silk thread comes from the spinnerets.

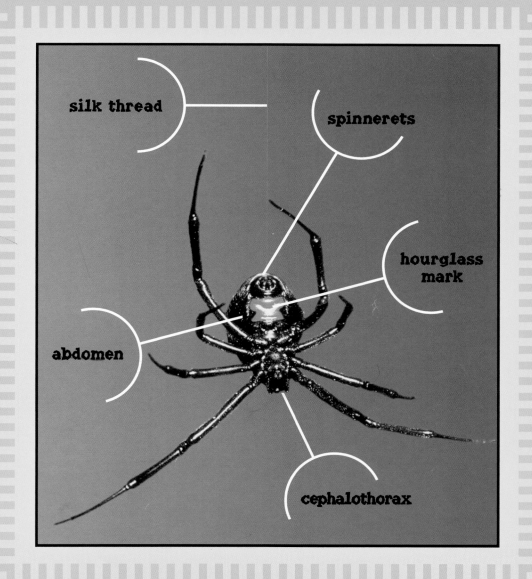

silk thread

spinnerets

hourglass mark

abdomen

cephalothorax

A spider can grow a new leg if it loses one.

Black widows handle prey with a pair of pedipalps. Pedipalps look like short legs. But they are more like feelers.

Black widows have seven joints in each of their eight legs. Joints allow a body part to bend. Your knee is a joint. Imagine having seven knees!

Feeding

A black widow uses her web to catch prey. She hangs upside down in the web with her belly facing up. Insects fly or crawl into the web and get stuck. These insects are the spider's prey. The spider will catch, bite, and wrap the prey in silk. The prey dies. Then, the black widow feeds by sucking on the prey. She sucks her food until it is dry.

This black widow spider has caught an insect in its web.

A black widow spider building its web.

Black widows eat centipedes and other arachnids, too. Some people believe the black widow female eats her mate. This is why this spider is called a black widow. A "widow" is a woman who has lost her husband by death.

A black widow spider and its prey.

Nests

Black widow spiders can live in hot and cool places. Mexico, Canada, and the United States have black widows. These arachnids stay in covered places that are dark and damp. Black widows might nest on the underside of plants or rocks. They try to stay hidden. You might find a black widow spider indoors, too.

Black widow spiders may nest in old wooden buildings like this one.

Spiderlings

Female black widows lay between 250 and 700 eggs at one time. She lays her eggs in a special egg sac. This silk egg sac keeps the eggs safe. Black widow eggs hatch after about 20 days.

The baby spiders, or spiderlings, stay inside the egg sac after hatching. There, the spiderlings can grow bigger. After many weeks the young spiders leave the egg sac.

A black widow spider and her egg sac.

Important Words

abdomen the back part of a spider's body.

arachnids small animals with two body parts and eight legs.

cephalothorax the front part of a spider's body.

pedipalps a spider's "feelers."

poisonous something full of poison. Poison is something that can hurt or kill you.

prey any living thing that is killed and eaten by another.

spinnerets the part of a spider's body that makes silk.

venom the poison spiders use to kill prey.

Web Sites

Up Close with Spiders

www.discovery.com/exp/spiders/upclose.html
Learn more about the body parts of a spider.

Spider Homepage

www.powerup.com.au/~glen/spider7.htm
This web site has information and pictures of
many common spiders.

Spiders of Northwest Europe

www.xs4all.nl/~ednieuw/Spiders/
spidhome.htm
Learn about spiders that live all over the world.

Index